THINGS THAT GO

LAURA EVE ENGEL

OCTOPUS
BOOKS

Things That Go
by Laura Eve Engel
© Copyright 2019
All Rights Reserved
Published by Octopus Books
Portland, OR
octopusbooks.net
Distributed by Small Press Distribution
spdbooks.org
ISBN : 978-0-9861811-8-4
First Printing
Cover design by Erik Carter
Design by AUTHENTIC

THINGS THAT GO

FURTHER PRAISE

Laura Eve Engel's supple, alert, dazzling, unpredictable poems are vibrantly alive: they turn and bend in daring and fantastic ways to access new angles of vision. *Things That Go* bristles with a verve that works to unsettle "the signage in our minds," expanding the seeable as these poems bring it unnervingly closer to the sayable. Engel knows "vigilance against the new appearance / of old growth / has never been enough / we must rewrite the ground." This book is that rewriting.

—Mary Szybist, author of *Incarnadine*,
2013 National Book Award winner

These poems exist in an eternal present, where one is continually in a state of waking. The waking is, often—movingly, thrillingly—into love. "First, building the love, which takes time. / Then making good of it, which takes forever." Wise and open, *Things That Go* is both knowing, and aware of the risks of knowing.

—Nick Flynn, author of *The Reenactments*

This long anticipated first collection from Laura Eve Engel is a remarkable debut! At its spine, *Things That Go* traffics in the collision of the sacred and the irreverent and paints a landscape of noticing where even static objects perceive deeply. The poems in this book carry such deft attention to sound, image, and sense, a reader might get lost in this book for hours. This is a collection to read, reread, and then read aloud to a friend.

—sam sax, author of *Bury It*

For Rozzy

CONTENTS

»

»

»

And when the morning arose, then the angels hastened Lot, saying:
'Arise, take thy wife, and thy two daughters that are here; lest thou be
swept away in the iniquity of the city.' [...] Then the Lord caused to
rain upon Sodom and upon Gomorrah brimstone and fire from the
Lord out of heaven; and He overthrew those cities, and all the Plain,
and all the inhabitants of the cities, and that which grew upon the
ground. But [Lot's] wife looked back from behind him, and she became
a pillar of salt.

Genesis 19–27

»

LOT'S WIFE

To be left to see all the way
to the end of it

to watch the sand burn
under a cloud growing dust
on the tables the rivers cut long
into the land

ice is an afterthought
cut and becoming

in this sudden heat

to have seen the land
reveal itself under a dark
thumb of weather

what must it be like
she thinks
to be weather

breath shaping the area
into portable plains

the horizon incises
seeable into a corner
of the eye

       sight

is a misformed feeling
placed in a pillar
of the body waiting
to become more of itself

piled into what it has seen
billowing like a dress
tears can crowd
the eye and freeze

a cataract of ideas
in the brimstone field

she's a painting of a feeling
that leaves her out
without name

to see tomorrow appear
like the sun
over time approaching

the clouds casting dark
animal shapes
on the clean terrain

to see without
violence is almost a name

»

Yellowed. Does forgetting have a color? Ah, this yellow, color of awakened sand.

Edmund Jabés

»

HOME ON THE RANGE

There are times where no one else exists.
They are more like places.

I love the great American west
where the moon hunts us
for a living.

It draws closer and then away from me.
Me! Where I cannot be stopped.

Under the moon's shadow stalk
where time encounters itself on the mesa
and is rubbed sandpapery by its own

imitable processes, I am
with an increasing frequency becoming.

I'm out thinking of wind
in a low presence of wind,

bending to stir the scrub and sage
that attends the heart's climb
from ridge to ridge.

Of feelings, of course.

The past must be a jerk, all those bonfires,
dead dogs, a herd of horizons
with me at its back. I nip and I nip.

And yet wherever I go I find myself
on my knees before a feeling so big
it's already been annexed

by the military. Being in love is like
almost knowing what is about to happen
before you are ripped apart by the sun
and its belly.

Like finally finding inside a haystack
there's a more beautiful
haystack.

From what did love all of a sudden
rear up? Or the knife

in my hand, where having one
means I believe in my life

in the language
of what it might become.

THE LAKE IS BURNING

To describe anything
is to imply a presence,

as in, there is within.

You are a warmth
the bad night draws itself around.

Light lands elsewhere,

makes a museum
of this flickering room where it was once
a topography of pleasures.

Today was a topography
of weather.

The wind,
the stance of the trees

arguing with chatter that moves
horizontally like traffic

over the event of people
moving toward their cars.

Conversation shares
almost nothing with the vertical trees,

more with cars moving toward their homes
where the light divides dinner
from its being eaten,

a set table still
in its intentions
from its intentions.

The meat is warm
and it is unmoving.

If anything's been learned today
about today,

whether or not the best part
is after cleaning up
after yourself without fanfare,

no one's saying.

Who sees water on its best
and only behavior moving
toward the lower ground.

You're never all the way into sleep
when the news arrives
and requires you.

If you're lucky it's an old love's arm
in your hair,

you're happiest
just before you know

the area around the lake is burning.

It's nothing like old bad love
everywhere
so warm you can see it,

but maybe a little like it too

far-off
and terrifying.

LOOK OUT, NATURAL DISASTERS ARE EVERYWHERE!

I was in the Rio Grande. It knocked me over.
I mean it knocked my breath around.
I was getting caught getting into something old.
Have you heard the one about the mountain
on the shore of the river that knocked its branches
into a deep green because it couldn't stand it?
It doesn't take hardly any time for me to forget
to consider there's a real need to stand it.
That lesson is far from me but not
like that mountain. Pictures of a river
on my phone remind me there are different kinds
of distance. If I can eat shit in the current
and also stay upright it gets into being two people.
Finally, a way to step in it twice.
For fun I try making travel plans without myself.
It's why we have two of every kind of animal.
She's somebody buying her ticket. I'm back
in the river, now a wooden beam, now a form
I would've told you I considered
too heavy to move.

AS IF IN A CAVE

School bus-bottled late light
of day, someone else's knees shoved
in your back, who knows how
your little tits might be growing
under there, kicking up through you
and into the air while you sit.
Who knows how it works.
The rest of you, a vine trained to run
along the ground. Your thighs flush
with the seat spread into afternoon
as geography, a new sea some
early people had to cross
to get to the part where history
starts. Weren't they fucking
impatient, sitting around waiting
to invent cookery, the calendar,
ships? A mapless people lolling
by the water on the rocks, each
desiring someone who'll really
treat her like a conqueror.
Your tiny new tits are slow
firecrackers. Science must be boring
if the whole world took so long
in getting to it. To spend the time
instead painting as if in a cave the word
for the feeling of being too big
for one's body on the bus, which is
the same as the word for always having
been there, which punches up
out of you now as if it's new life.

PEOPLE WITH NOTHING TO SAY
SAY PLENTY TO THE DOG

Today the trees fill the space
I might fill saying *today the trees*.
A whole stand of them laps

at the horizon. It's a morning
I have a feeling we keep walking
into the same morning

or that I meant to say waking
and we must always say
we say what we mean.

The dog's bowl empties at a speed
that's alarming. The dog empties
its bowl and who cares how fast.

This won't be the same as what
we want to say or trees so say
today's when we say what we can

on a day with weather or in a room
with a dog, then put whatever's left
out in a box I can keep on making

boxes out of. The dog has its blank dog-
thoughts we feel free to put a thing or two
inside of, like *look at me being a dog*

I'm a dog dog dog I have some teeth I'd like
to show you is one way we can throw
our voices. Away towards trees is another.

FOR THE SAKE OF THE HEART WE SACRIFICE THE HEART

Under a sun   I am not permitted to name

all the shedding stars   between the piñon

light sits like a bird at church   a song straight and quiet as salt

taken from the land   poured into the glittering land

if the soul needs solitude   canyon-muscled

as the tree needs room to grow   gutted by mesas

the thin air makes a lie impossible   titanic moon

low on discreet green fields   like the cactus in winter

we may be afraid to grow   any quieter we'll forget

the blast   old wounds in the mind of the land

we are rarely a witness   to a good story

we live inside our story   where we're the hero

humans we turn to watch   obliterated in the blast

the bad idea of justice   we can be certain

includes us growing still   beside a past we can no longer claim

the one in the desert   was ours straight and white as salt

we don't know how to name   gypsum maybe white sands

from space a small scar's on the earth   Mars has one that matches

what we have here is an effort   to put stories together

salt in the desert   a pillar of salt in the mind

of the desert   that stilled me before I was

THE LIGHTNING FIELD

*

In the desert there's a field where people go to be beside themselves waiting
for lightning. To wait for the lightning in a field sewn with metal poles.

I have this only kind of visual idea. In it I'm a pole
that waits for a real feeling to pull in a downward motion towards me
like a tapestry or sword.

I collect the times during a day I pretend to be in the act of knowing.
In what I become while in the act of knowing, I am urgent, like a pole.

All day warnings have been wringing out the flat grey air but I know
what the weatherman is really saying:
that I may be a monument to my own investigating whatever I want.

The weather is a worthy adversary,
it knows what it'll all be like come morning.

But it's here one way or the other, this lightning field in the desert mallow.

But ever I am arriving at the present moment bearing a great distance in mind.

*

Even inside this sense of the great elemental there's time to be a tourist.

I can remember every time another person's asked me if I'm doing okay
while I'm chugging a large container of diet soda. In my element.

And I can always be okay in a carnival kind of situation.

There's even time to think of love, though perhaps this isn't. I can eat a corndog.

Who was it who said no matter where you are you can always smell
the smell of the sea?

When in a fish-out-of-water-type state a person will sometimes say
no matter where she is she can always smell
the smell of the sea. Quote it too burns the edges of the land end quote.

*

When there are no people for miles my heart slows for the sand
which is granular and invisible unless there's a lot of it in one place like people.

Before I arrived there were two of me in the car.
Here I am, eager to discover the site of a future splitting
the sky into its parts.

To what do I owe the pleasure? I think at the shadows explaining the shifting sky.
It bears the mark of outside forces,

the decisions of wind projected on sand, the tiny weatherman living
in what I know whenever I know anything about the weather.

There come with the body and the moment of course all kinds of limitations.
Having only one of them, for example,
and the issue of where they go when I'm not looking.

Sometimes I call things other than what they are but maybe
in the morning I will once again escape blame.

*

My involvement with the lightning field isn't straightforward.
Like the evening, evenly spaced over the mesa, a combination of time and events
delivered me.

I'm looking to be planted evenly in the deep evening, then reached for
by the warm sum of its details.

Could a pane of glass come to rest evenly on these details?
Their origins, concrete among the aster.

Apricot mallow, purple aster, broom—anyway, there must be a light that cries out
to be carried from one place to another by what you see
is possible.

When my mind bends again towards the sky it's barely a skin
on this earth, just a thought remaining of the old books all together.

*

When I can barely remember the desert I can remember
I lost the urge to see my own face

and that the lightning field did not find me buried like an egg
under a warm heavy sky and lift me up.

Taking aim over the long held breath of the plain, it didn't river down,
transform the ground into golden soldiers.

Light makes the desert look like the known desert.

Illuminated on the plain in a series of events
that refuses to conform to my sense of how long an observed event should last,
the white dunes crest the view.

Something known is locked inside my body.

*

My favorite part about the tenderness part is that it is unnecessary.

Often it's proper to think of an ending, then start there.
This isn't the hard part. No one's saying what that is.

A sky grown half wild as if with hair makes the mind red.
I've gone desperate wild or I don't mind the tenderness present

in saying it, like gawking from the car at too many cows in one pen
makes me sad on the long drive away from the lightning field.

Too many cows grazing openly will resist this little inference
about suffering. The old heifers were never wrong either.

Where reason the color of hay may burst open near the road,
the hay light spilling open, any moment may be the one where I catch myself

beside what I went into that field for, and would again.
Not today. There are so many different instances of time

in one animal. Like an unvisited thought a voice suddenly breaks through
and tumbles towards the ground. It could be mine.

»

I couldn't breathe and spun around and around.
Anyone who saw me must have thought I was dancing.
It's not inconceivable that my eyes were open.
It's possible I fell facing the city.

Wislawa Szymborska, "Lot's Wife"

»

LOT'S WIFE

Camille Corot, "The Burning of Sodom," 1843, oil on canvas

He paints her tenderness
as a black shroud unsexed
in the right-hand corner
of the painting pregnant
with shadow under the hand
of a red event
   to have lost it all
to a small distance
moving in the neck
blooming from the middle
of the body like a fish
rising into the dream
of the water hunt
   for her daughters
what's left of a city
turns to ice before turning
back to the river a new city
forming around the chutes
of an old way of seeing
   to introduce their eyes
to the juniper growing into
the lightning in the field
they bear each other
away on the lit plain
   as the painter shepherds
weather around her
dark shoulders she exists only
as oil ready to burn

if ever he found
this painted city
its actual canvas
in flames
she is the one—he
admitted—he would turn back
himself to save

FRAMES

Say we begin with things
       I say I see
there's a house

then to smooth out the part
       where I think
I'm not being clear

I cut my bangs to see
       clearly more
over there

so that house
       will look less
like a house

with hair out front
       I can sit here
with this face to try

to make my looking clear
       looking's hard
to look like

from possible faces
       I can choose squint
which is narrow

and hurts and things
        are lost
in the vision field

who made vision
        a field
who built that house

to look like a house
        with bangs
in the way

say I address you
        sometimes-curator
of the unmown yard

or whatever
        say I tell you
I see but what for

is a way to get at
        you saw dandelions
when I said field

and meant buildings

VIEW FROM HERE

Reflections of my favorite buildings
on the water waver,
look up at me with a sadness.

The sun readies itself for today's tourists
and costs nothing.

On the eleventh floor
working away at my things, I cost a little bit,
even though mostly my things are wondering

why we say floor when we mean to say
this building lets us work away at our things
from the sky—the sky!—

with pretty much impunity.
Meaning I get to walk around most days
not noticing I'm not falling

so I'm free to notice how the lake catches
and then makes tremble every last solid it sees.

When I hear that some others are unhappy
with maintaining the road I take

to get here I want to say *Who pumped you*
so full of melancholy
and fed you to the barnyard animals?

Haven't you noticed we're up in the sky?

IF NOT BY SMOKESTACK

A girl may not be meant
        to think of her mouth
as a smokestack but insists

are you sure we're still moving is a feeling
        and that feeling chuffs like a train
until delay, when sorry opens

panoramic in her body as opens up
        this track first to hauling freight.
Now calls for a telling, meaning

why did she lift the cup
        there at that moment and then
set it down in that way,

or does it mean what train
        was she waiting on when,
or more likely yes it's been a long time

since smokestacks, etc. She lifts
        the cup or sets it down,
still nothing goes.

Still turns the train to platform.

       What starts with a mouth

and a girl thinking smokestack

won't stay put. When we say about

       the cup we're never sure

it could mean we're waiting

to be a part of something

       moving. If not by smokestack then

to be made a girl, to be made

to fashion something

       about mouths or locomotives

more accurately is a way,

if old, of going forward. If

       for chuff. If to make seeable

how this heading somewhere used to go.

TO GO ONE WAY IS A THING WITH DOORS

To go one way is a thing　　　　　with doors

the hinge makes a way　　　its flapping reckless

the garden leans heavy　　　its wants on the trellis

in its ivy the house　　　full of its objects

everything's divided　　　　yard into its grass

the cut carrots divided　　　knives from their reflections

the fan marshals the air　　　a series of slices

everything moving　　away from itself

all on its hinges　　inches away

two big boots leave　　　a missing feet shape

a rip turns a shape　　to a shape of itself

my mouth turns a name　　　to a sound my mouth owns

a person leaves　　　the split shape of a person

the split shape of a person　　　a person inhabits

it's one way with doors　　　behind them are others

the not-knowing chews me　　　so I will say others

DEFINED CONTRIBUTION

I'm in the park without my glasses wondering
why the park doesn't feel more betrayed.
If I were that sign over there I'd be angrier.
If I were that sign I don't know what
I would say. Everyone here has thoughts
about what everyone else should be doing
while I push food around on this paper plate
until it spells out *I dare you to take off my shirt.*
It's true that I only want to feel it on my neck
until it covers my whole face. I don't care what
happens after. It's true too that sometimes I want
to stop looking altogether but I can't, I'm waiting
for those moments when a city rising clearly up
out of the ground is so beautiful I think
that it must have been a part of the earth
until God or something like it shook it—
the earth   until its lesser parts just fell away.
I know what's built is built by people. I know
that to call this kind of knowing *knowledge* isn't.
As a basket fills it tilts towards being made
more of what's inside it, until basket becomes
cheese, and bread, and bread. Maybe on the days
we can't be stopped it's that we're not done
making something like ourselves of this park.
Today I'm putting it all towards counting
on the nearby trees, how without destruction
they grow ever outward, to instruct me.

PARTICULAR DISTRICT

A tree is always inhabiting itself is why we invoke it.
Too thick for even a throat of light to sift through.
Separated from the city's little lights by water,
it's always snowing somewhere at the same time
it isn't somewhere else. The forest has its chalice
of sky to swish. Awe is a technology that reinvents
itself. *Than ever before* happens over and over.
Pushed out past the margins of the forest standing in
for a hard dark where we're more afraid than ever
before to go, a tree begins to look like a district.
Then, ever before is over. Woodedness, a shark-
toothy find in a city, breaks away from our usual
all-at-once at the same time a building on mooned water
is both one thing and split. Here and now is the part
where the light lifts out of the roots of the city's
own image and the part where the light is lifting it.

TOWARDS BLUEPRINT

If no one's going to come over here
                I don't feel much like drinking
      is a good way to stay sober
                    makes sober-
thoughts appear like a train moves along
              tracks it doesn't own itself
      and for this reason is never on
                    time with its way
of arriving and making itself clear even
      as over the phone a voice
says I'm getting the hang
        of chess by which
      the voice means moving
and then it says moving
                and I hear sadness
      isn't at all like most buildings
you can't go to a government
      office and roll out
        the plans we made
out of a sense that there had to be sense
        it made sense that way
      until they started to look too much like

plans made for downtown buildings
            demonstrate a particular kind of
                              growth disturbing
the stuff around the spot where the most of it
                        happens
                  when blowing a hole
        in the side of a mountain makes
a mountain of a different sort
                              it edges into place
                  if mountains edge
            or if between us is a place
                              I'd like
to put some things like my hand
                        on your hand
            though I give it no permission
will be the one thing I'm likely to remember about
                  the sleeping
            trainyard carries a wide space
for a whistle even when it is still
                  its shape like a mouth pushing air
            working into a whistle we can teach
                              ourselves how
                  or we can pucker
a little before giving up makes our faces
                        a little soft

                    a good quality in the ground
               if you plan to plant
          but not for building
buildings is a way to fill the sky with things
                                        to look at for example
             there's a line we refer to
and are proud of like it is the most
                         important shape of our city
          relief of this big important
city rising up out of its plans
                         at a speed I could bring back
          the trains and their speed we used to talk
about survival as a thing with which
                              we are all a bit concerned
          is how I'll say I'm afraid I can't
see the sun today and my eyes are fine
               instruments to be able to tell
          how big this is getting in its own
                              way and giving way
                    to when
we look to the drawing up
               of our plans we won't see past
the building we might have hoped to be there
               when we got done putting it to
                         this big blue unfurling

CALENDAR YEAR

Pre-arrangements this time have been made to keep a close
watch on the way we've kept track of our sentences exactly.
It's time we broke out some qualifying language with

precision and were friendly-like. It's time in the morning
the trash truck reminds me to be better about how
I will remember the cans. To the curb is where I will

never have the wherewithal on the right day to drag them.
What marks my memory of the right day on the day
before the day. Where's the posted up reminder.

Some minds come with signage to designate
all the important deadlines and some of us stack all
of the unbuilt bookshelves' shelves in a pile and pile

the books on top. To see the one you want most
naked is a relief like something organized, like building
buildings gives a skyline a sense of itself and we in a city

are pleased. We in a city say please us and turn on
the radio to get a taste of something like regularly
scheduled. I'm talking about calling on us to come back

to taping our favorite tunes. On a day in July I brought
tapes to the fireworks display to introduce what I loved
to the sky showing off what it does to us in our ears.

What a good bottle does to the song in our chest.
When no one else appears to be listening here's some
big thing we can share. Look over there while I say that

seasonal weather comes in a handmade envelope like mix
tapes on the days we staked out the lockers of the ones
we thought we somehow and like music wanted to take

into our bodies. I'm exhausted keeping track of the days
unrelated to everything makes me think my teeth are
falling out. Nothing says pens for public use like chains

ensure the dead ones are always the most available. Nothing
says leaving's an expensive choice like a cab. Nothing says
more light like I love you. The road at night is the same

at any temperature. We'll wait until we're looking forward
to waiting is too neatly wrapped to be accurate is what we're
after when we decide again whether or not to hit the bars.

We get upset. We turn over all the plants in the house
to get whatever needs to be gotten to their roots but we're
bad at interpreting directions. The floor is where we'll place

our only hammock. Next year is how the trampoline will go.
Neighborhoods remind us that monkey bars are treacherous
and monkey bars remind us slides are heavenly as long as we

can keep the babies where we like to see them and from falling off. A limit and a way is what we have. Seasons. Marking time until the marked-off time is right.

OBSERVATION CAR

A train makes a sound like I don't
know what to call it when things

are approximate. I lean forward
in my seat and I am a lot like

my leaning. You are a lot like I'd like
to be telling you that staying always

outside this train is something the
other train is good at. We're all good

at thinking the other one's moving
is maybe what this train is trying to

tell us we don't know if the mountains
we're seeing are good at anything more

than waiting by us to be seen. Your body,
something I miss like a window.

All around me there's
a present correctness
and the crumbling.
Those muscular birds
look like they belong
to the sea. They are
making everyone
nervous. I've gathered
my ethics into a small
stone pile. For maybe
a second I get it, the
whatever about birds
that makes them little
suitcases, only it goes
like *What makes us
want to stuff our ideas
about beauty inside
them.* Then I think
that I must be in love.
To let just anything
in like that. I'm
worried. A grown-
up woman eats
candy for breakfast
on the train and order
begins to fall apart
like teeth. These
sightings I've been
collecting and care

nothing for. We do
what we want. Soon
I'll watch a different set
of movements altogether
and I don't even have
to plan it. A thought
about what's happening
has nowhere to be.
When the lady
in the train station
tells me *You don't judge,*
you don't judge a person
until you step on his shoes,
it stays there.

DEBT

I mean to develop a formula for what's spent
mid-afternoon developing formulae at the desk—
contract, reduction, velocity, no velocity, drug,
unwashed corners, the door—but today drags itself
ahead of itself. Today rolls around and I
at the helm of my chair-ship expand at the site
of whatever news until it's impossible to locate a center
of this kind of inattention must have a name.
I mean to find a worthy place to sit. Once
I saw the capitol building from a place in the sky.
My error was in describing something so ordinary.
Now you won't sleep with me. You tell me I smell
like I print my own money. It's like what they say
about giving birth, it misplaces the wonder.
Or maybe it's that nobody's interested in the rain
we're going to have until it's upon us. Or that the sky's
too dark for worry. Mostly I worry about being
in the wrong place with my hands full, about the dark,
about how when it's time I'll haul it all back.

I WILL MAKE A USEFUL MANUAL FOR MY TASKS AND HIDE IT

I don't owe anybody for the bad thoughts I think
or will think. It isn't right, the access this gives me
to everything. A person with actual access has access
to knives but not necessarily ways to make more knives.
To make more of anything one must go a long way
across a great distance, past symbolic trees and lush
ideas of desert, fences, all the way to where the blades
just glint up out of the land and are more or less ripe
for the plucking. More or less was never an actual
question. When there's more weather outside than
inside a building, the building's windows spring
big glassy tears. I don't see what good it does,
putting it this way. Ours is a history of a breathing
building letting people go to prove it breathes.
I'm at work in a building where I draw strange birds
to scale, where down the hall a man comes in every day
and remembers one day in December in his childhood
for a living until one day he doesn't. Sometimes the sky
just opens up. Not everything's allowed. Nobody,
for instance, cares very much for my singing voice
but I can spell *daffodil* however I want. I want to say
I see a great many possibilities for development around
the office, which I will call recognizing our potential,
which I will call *daffodil*, which is why you'll keep me
for as long as you can, like a pleasant taste at the end
of a meal. This new thing our building's about to be
about has many spellings I'll travel distances for.

INDUSTRIAL COTTAGE

*

From the middle, you can see a tower.

No money in the mug.
A more affordable medicine under the mattress, no.
There's the door.

When in the morning the stampede of metal hits the earth,
when it troubles the underearth with its teeth, none of it is paint.
Skim of your breastbone, none of it.

Steam rises up out of the work like more work.

*

In the opposite of woods, in the red ever, I am hungry and you are.

I used to have this job, the bodies entered all at once in a line,
towing their essentials.
Men left, as I, it's hard to say whether it was for love.

Now I enter the sky alone, paint anything
that can make a man look up from his driving.

*

One need not have an actual pig pressed into his mind in order to have a mind of bacon
is a principle I cling to when hanging from a billboard's girders.

Suggest, suggest largely.

On his way home from the office, a man calls his love.
He's just seen a new way to make their home better and it's only 50′ tall.

If you look closely there's a little someone flapping from each billboard like a flag.
Like the calm after the application but before that next moment.

A particular method of extinction by hope.

I used to sidle up to the wall, stall there and curl. Wait for you to come home.

Paint your shadow in the doorway for you to step into and delight,
small and smelling like a coin behind each ear.

*

everything all	*hung out*
in the dark	*of the work*
you've seen	*at that hour*
there are fewer of you	*lights on the road*
many of me	*pocketing*
the air	*as I climb*
to paint to sell	*to paint*
in sunrise	*the new billboard*
divides the sky	*from itself*
and until	*it has replaced*
all moments	*after*

*

At quitting time the factory of me all bursts apart.

Until then, I'm forced to consider how the function of the individual screw
may be beauty, balletic.

The drill bit in its business of displacement sends up into the air a fine spray.
What's left can't afford to stay.

I can't account for when in the day my hair moves,
and yet it tumbles from this to this.

And yet I am away from you badly.
It itches, to be gone, and I am poor from it.

*

You have not been made of flowers.

Architecture I loved, I should have been.
I've always had a spark for a fine building.

You rest in an angle of our home, functional,
where I am permitted to notice.

You are, and are held up by it as time eats the ridge's edge.
As I am held up by your color in flower pressed in mind.

When a man remarks on a quality of a building
it is mercy that allows him to use his own mouth.

*

In sun when it mallets one side of the toolbelt I'm under I'm earning my pleasure.
I'm earning the smile I'll spend on you after, watching you tear into the rabbit.

Butter, mustard, tarragon, we secreted away the rabbit in the sock drawer,
we spent the very idea of it, we turned the room over when we thought it lost,
we turned each other out, we overdrew, we sent it down our throats.

*

It opens on a tower, the middle, which has showcased repeated arrivals of the loved one
in the driveway. The scrape her body makes. The sun's many movements.

A window used to be used to say *soul*. Say *eyes* and be enveloped by the odor.
Would you get close enough to a painted sign to smell it?
It is a windowless room when you put it like that, its fumes swaddling the brain organ.

For how the window frames my coming home to your dismantling of meat,
I tell you, I would anything, would turn myself out.

*

Night enters like a drill bit.

The last dust of day's sky's pitched, dark having rubbed the it out of it.

A long, smart swath of black on trees, efficiently employed.

Now here is a palate that turns the mind to commerce,
beyond where what we might say about what's beyond the window, love, the rabbit, is.

This slow skid from metal to ash, and you: that, I, for the whole sold world, call tender.

ESCAPE HATCH

Was thinking escape hatch is what I'd require.
I think *escape hatch* to myself in the park
and see it slink on its two good legs away
from view, leaving me with this turned-
over feeling. So long, hatch. Hello.
For a while now I've been hiding the news
from myself, but sometimes thoughts
try to locate the exits while I'm sleeping.
I wake to the notion of taking someone's hands
in my hands putting on its shoes in the dark,
making its way to the door. Come back,
hands in my hands. Sometimes my thoughts
ask for gratitude and I become furious.
As far as I know, thoughts, cancer still exists,
and math, and you, like a shovel, have done
about what you can do with these things
and no better. Mostly what you've done is
a little light soil reorganization. My confusion
this time has to do with how routinely
we pick up handfuls of shore and toss them
into the water like we don't know what
we're doing. The world is full of containers
waiting to be spilled out or stepped into
like a sandbox, supported for the moment
by so many tiny plastic tractors. I hold
my phone up to the sun and it is in this way
that I live on the backs of other, loftier ideas.
Then there are geese and I point at them
as if I've been asked to prove it, their sounds

and that letter in the sky they swallow into.
As around everything the world is gestured at
and goes on, I've been made by those two
distant buildings, how they face one another
and do not move, to feel like a coward.

»

Pray for the welfare of the Government, for if people did not fear it,
they would swallow each other alive.

Rabbi Haninah, Pirkei Avot

»

LOT'S WIFE

A small accident
in a white mound
overclothed
below a cloud wisp
tucked behind an ear
of mountain
where the lilac's
overgrown
effigies arrive
singular like ideas
a frame of hands
crosses the desert
like a painting
that tells you
where you are
is a mesa
you've been brought
to the edge of
knowing to watch
the mushroom
cloud the sand
salt cedar filling
with omen
if you outlive
the fire if you can
stand to outlive it
what will you call
yourself

I CAN WATCH A MAN IN A CAGE GET BURNED ALIVE

Muath Safi Yousef al-Kasasbeh, 1988-2015

I can watch a man in a cage get burned alive.

I can watch his raised hands join at his forehead.

I can speculate about a body in prayer.

I can watch the orange of his jumpsuit go up.

His face, I can make comparisons. I can turn the sound up or off.

I can constitutes the first half of a decision
which is often followed by additional considerations and time.

It involves the weighing of his hands
against alive, against my hands,

a speculation about orange, the jumpsuit, the raised cage.

If I can watch an orange prayer go up in a man's body
I can never unwatch it.

A speculation about who I will be, then. After.

It's how time works. It doesn't stop working.

Sometimes I can't do what I can.

BURDEN OF BELONGING

Inauguration Day, January 20, 2017

Today we are grieving our nation's
peaceful transition of power

what we are really saying is we're scared
about how many of us
choose not to recognize
we depend on one another

to stay whole and unhurt

I am responsible for you
here   hold my heart

why am I glad for this burden
of belonging when others
are not

to whom do some of us
not belong
who hurt some of us so

but here they come again
this history of men

who when they were healthy
refused the hearts of their neighbors
until they were weak from it

now their suffering punches up
out of the rich soil

thorny and asserting
you are not suffering I am
suffering

something inside the weed
urges it to need
and kill the garden

to offer and offer itself
until it's choked all
but its own color out

where it was never written
not all suffering is created equal
and not all need

vigilance against the new appearance
of old growth
has never been enough

we must rewrite the ground

A PROBLEM WITH THE MOON IN IT
IS THE SKY

Suppose the moon was falling right out of the sky.
Suppose it was headed on a steady course
straight for me, as when sometimes through a trick
of depth my perception fails and it looks to be.
Suppose I choose to stand right under it saying
Fuck you, moon. My friend is dead. I stay up
and cuss at the moon. It's a lot of good I'm doing.
My anger doesn't know what it's doing
but one possibility is that it's making the moon
bigger and bigger until it's too heavy to stay put.
Tonight the air is wet, everything still alive
smudged by a strong thumb of moonlight.
Suppose this is one answer to a problem that goes
if I climb the tallest mountain where I live
and you're still dead, how long will it take me
to remember to be grateful for both my legs.
If this is an answer and a new question comes up
over those hills and sets itself down in these trees
like a squatter the trees will have to deal with
forever how come I never even got to see you leave.
I'd like to be crushed or made whole by a force
greater than the handful of facts I cling to
on a cold evening, oriented not even a little
by the stars, less by the emerging landscape
of nighttime creatures that beg for a little
less noise, please, from me. Their small bodies
finally powerful in the uncertain dark.
Once we had a staring contest with the moon.
It shut up like it knew its place. It hung open

like an unsaid thought. Why shouldn't it take
the long ride down to me now, batter me
into the leaves, me and all the timid animals
in the leaves, unburdened of its light
and under its own weight suddenly endless.

MEMORIAL DAY

In front of me the apple tree
is ordered. It has leaves
on its leaf parts. I say it sits
and it sits, fulfilling its
treeness as surely as it never
reads the news. I'd like
to read it the news.
Good morning, apple tree,
the morning your air's in
is in memorial. Hello, morning,
your young men are on fire
with bad ideas. Your guns
are growing into their gun
parts. And now more thoughts
arrive, disguised as this yellow
butterfly taking the act of flying
for granted as surely as I
have been unfair to young men
and that this will continue.
Today we celebrate
the apportioned dead, some
of whom were poured
on their alive mornings
into the bodies of young men.
Soldiers. The leaves strain in their
leaf parts, here, and in the town
I drove past to get to the tree
I'm at, town with *those dead*
children poured inside

its name. I say *it* and it
can be any one of. Inside
and outside of a young man
and me the old air turns. It turns
beside our instruments.
A mind in its child parts.
The day threatening
to grow into itself.

ALL THE SCIENCES

The year I fail all the sciences there are
many factors but no one is in any way confused.
The radio brimming with everything it knows
about some shooters until it gets the shooters
down to two. The dead men's rooms reveal
nothing about unhappiness. What starts out
as reason refusing to make more of itself
has a way of becoming several mixed reports
from the field, where I'm having a feeling
of being eleven and watching the sun set.
I'm having a feeling of my chest as a trunk
full of blankets and answers to questions
about who gets to keep a garden. Often
enough we return to the field with trowels,
intentional. I'm told this is an American
approach to the problem. I've been trying
to figure out what it means to have
an American approach to a problem.
Maybe it's when I think the thoughts I have
that don't work hard enough to stick
probably weren't deserving of the field,
and not when I think the ones that do
are lucky. We like to be told what we're doing
is difficult so it's correct that the sky's mostly
a flubbed forecast until the part where it turns
to light or to egg down the calm sides
of a mixing bowl. I remember that to make
a solution, something needs to dissolve.
Sunsets. The library. The parts we've picked

apart with borrowed beaks or tractors.
It feels good to get an old thing next to
a new thing because of how sure it is
that they'll never turn into each other, or
maybe it's because we like what putting a rock
near a rocket says about what we can do
in the meantime. Sometimes I like to read
backwards until the bullet reenters its gun.
Until the dead men remove their heads
from the bags and are about to be
hungry or can almost remember what
they came into that room for or are born.

APPLE-SHOT

Watch me, I'm like Newton
before he had his big idea,
just a body looking around
for something to eat. Suddenly
it's clear: how it all falls.
How history pulls us all,
a little lonely, towards it.
Sometimes, a little without
remorse. Here I am, these
two bolts for my crossbow
and no child to threaten
or save, still on the prowl
for some rich fruit to split
in two with my accuracy.
Or else, defend. Or use
to describe my predicament,
get myself banned forever
from the garden. I'm afraid
I'm no good defense against
anything: not the weeds
gone wild in the garden,
not the blades hidden in their
apple costumes, not our ancestry.
A girl full of apples is nothing
but a girl and a belly and
a concern for how things
will shake out. How can I
ever be two enough to eat
and eat?

MY NEW GRIEF

If there is new grief

if it isn't just the shadow

of that old known future arriving

my new grief returns as a rooster

in the kicked up leaves it yells

Make way for my new grief!

I am a house full of alarm clocks

therefore a rooster is ridiculous

the morning is ridiculous clownish

the sun breathing ground into gold

like it just learned how

and I know nothing

like it's something I own

MANUFACTURING

You slap one spider dead.
Now you have a bed full
of imaginary biting bugs.

Thought making the thing
on the skin. The thought
of the thing, you try saying

out a name in almost-sleep
with one hand down
the pants. Make the thought,

trick the skin. Or was it
the thing. A bed still
with bugs inside it. Please,

you say, on the skin. Make
the thought. Not this, please,
the other thing. The other

thought, skin. See how you
pull the covers back to nothing,
how there aren't even bugs.

The thing on the skin makes
the thought. At some point
it had to have been there.

Insect, little limbs.
The bite first. Then
these mind-made stings.

A MUSEUM IS ROOMS

Maybe being in the presence of great effort
will make me great. I make a mess
of myself to get to the museum, where
a photograph is an object about being
observed in a comfortable temperature.
I don't need to describe these walls
to you, and yet here is a color for making way
for other people's thoughts. *I couldn't
get it up to go to the party. I am a bag of leaves.*
One photograph is an object about a man
with the ghost of an old town in his hands.
The ghost of a love long gone from him
who says *But if I make sense to you, and yet
I must not be done growing.* I move towards him
as if I'd offer something about how precise
the angle of shadow, about contrast,
or how great we might die. How full
of definitions. A museum is rooms
where thinking approaches other thinking
like it might be a bear. Often it is full
of the French. Germans. Thought
approaching thought in a bunch of languages.
I know one language. I used a bunch of it
to speak to you but not to compliment
you in your shirt. *Purple looks good on everyone.*
I used my one language to say that.

YOU LOVE DESPERATELY AND LIKE A RAFT

You love desperately and like a raft
the clear water that holds up your boat.
The water was clearly built to buoy the boat.
It's like how TV shows buoy the dead.
After they've died, there they are,
their kind faces float just out of reach
like a rescue. Like that tiny island.
I promise I'm not making this up.
Today the world is full of people
who are dead and also you are in it.
By all accounts, everyone everywhere
should be drowning, there's tons
of water all over and only a few ideas
about how to stay dry and out of it.
From your raft the smell of the water
is patient, which for now is enough
to love it, which for now is helping.

»

Don't let my sorrow
make evil of me.

Tony Kushner, "Lot's Wife"

»

LOT'S WIFE

A man's back when he sleeps
beside me in the small bed
resembles him

a righteous stone
he grows against me like green to a river

I am a river of stone

I drive deep into the bedrock
into the heart of the desert

carrying him
his steps on my back
a strong scaffold

in the home

there's no room for god
beside the solid breath of god

and yet I am a promise to bring myself
wherever I go

even as I sleep I am driving away from him
towards an empty rain
a gypsum plain

the bite of wind
that makes the dunes each night
without faith or need

what's inevitable doesn't require speed

not even movement

the insinuation that to change
location means one foot in front
of the other

two feet inside the car

sometimes to leave you just stay
where you are

FOR YOU OUT OF SOFT MATERIALS

It's summer and the bodies fling sweat at each other.

The park is jammed with people
at work blocking the sun. A boy throws a ball
in a way that's American.

Once in a park you cupped my cheek and said
now don't think I'm cupping your cheek.

Time goes like all those people and then all these people.

Someone calls a dog a cupcake
and someone calls back *you're being absurd.*

Once I admitted I made my face
for you out of soft materials,
so you'd have a place to put all your fingers.

Probably it was wrong of me.
It's a good day for a joke. Tell me the one

whose punch line is platypus, then I'll say
platypus is a joke whose punch line is platypus.

Look, the little lusts diffuse
in a gust like a thing we could wish on.

There are all these ways
we can decide not to be very tender.

FIRST, BUILDING

In my new room where someone scrawled
on the wall *I love yoe for evry ting you do* it's hard to feel
like a victim. I have a bathtub to have my thoughts
inside. A window on the dreary side of the day
that eases into something like light. The air.
I've lost track of why I do this but recall
just enough to watch the news closely
for an answer. My hands, which smell like air,
which smells like fish, come up with little.
Bags. No job, I made moving to this room
a job. Where the air hasn't come in contact
with your air, which smells like hands. The news
says less people are not going to work now
than in a while. Less of me hasn't gone
to the park today than yesterday. Magnanimous
in the park, I call an old friend thinking it's
magnanimous but it turns out that isn't what's
required. What is required? And is it love
for all I don't know in the world that keeps me
slowly at it. First, building the love, which takes time.
Then making good of it, which takes forever.

UPKEEP

I'd never hurt another person
on purpose but to think that I could has a smell
and it's in my kitchen and there are flies.

How I've missed you is one thing I can say
again to trash day as I read articles
about someday being in rooms where sitting

on the floor doesn't mean now it's time to focus
on my breathing until I'm sure the floor isn't
going anywhere. I'm sure the floor isn't going

anywhere the walls aren't going with it
by which I mean I need to be focusing
on the way my chest can, when I'm doing this

right, bloat up like a sail. Everything needs
to stop being symbolic so take out the trash
can mean take out the trash and done can be

what it means when I've done it.
The empty curb yawns, appears huge,
and what wrong I may have done already

rings out like a frying pan to the ear,
where one would be remiss when taking
a frying pan to the ear to think only

of breakfast. Look how a beautifully fried
pair of eggs can become the only smell
becomes a kind of managing.

WHEN YOU KNOW YOU'RE GOING TO DIE IT'S DIFFICULT TO BEHAVE YOURSELF

Here in the form of hair and language only, I want to talk to you a minute.

In the morning in the mountains, they're awash in their colors as if nothing is ever sad.

I'm putting it together: that caring for other people isn't the same thing as knowing where they are.

The long-for-this-world-ness building in our names and hair.

One way to contain forest fires is to set fire to a far off stand of trees before it burns.

And the days beep on.

One of the buttons on my shirt pops open without history but not without meaning.

And aren't we all going to be if we aren't already outliving the people we love.

People insist on celebrating their love outdoors the way people insist on celebrating their love.

A log of sunlight rolls past on its way to the river, which is on its way in a kind of hurry.

The day seems to like where it is.

And yet leaving you is like sticking my tongue out at the ocean.

And yet leaving you is like you leaving me.

RECIPROCITY

And who bites who for a living.
And who skims the scrape off whose knee.
And who warm milks who into evening.
And who pops whose blister, the skin bright for popping.
And who shields who from the shadow's big tree.
And who bends whose face into a picture of sadness.
And who hangs the frame in place on the wall
and who watches and helps with the crooked.
And who makes the coffee and whose mouth does it burn.
And whose mouth falls apart from the burn and who kisses it.
And who builds up the show with its shiny guitars and who stays home.
And who whines like a bird and who like a toothache.
And who blames it on distance and who on the front yard.
And who sends who to the bottom of a sweet drink.
And who shames who into yes-making.
And who cops a feel and who an out.
And who talks to the weather and who to the dog.
And who to the dog says who took him out last time.
And who sees the news and who thinks it's about who.
And who lights some matches to flick them at who.
And who makes a noise like the time who was crying.
And who cries for who and who cries for who.

SOMETHING BLUE

Two people I love are parting. I left
my shoes in the desert. Maybe I'm like
a wedding, I have a formal need to make
these two ideas meet, the colors of each one
meeting, as if in a vineyard they are to be made
better by each other. I'm not like a vineyard.
The last time I started out with an idea
I looked out across the water until the idea
chimneyed up out of me and away. That's
how I know it feels good to give yourself up
over something blue. So what if each day
absence shakes me down to my toes, bare
now and which have never left the earth,
which have always dug down deep
into this earth. One way of learning
that the sky lights up is saying it.
Another is going back to the desert
to find you. When this new thirst appears
in the canyon of my throat I'm all hands
in the bucket, channeling my this is how
I have been taught to handle it feeling.
I don't have to fight to make this body
any more strange. Far away, two people
I love are parting, and their belongings,
and a man believes his grief cares for him
enough to follow him wherever he goes
like a beloved. Nothing takes as long as loving
and unloving. Lightning, distance, I can see
my feet won't tell me if the storm
I see from here is going to be coming.

MY BODY IS AFRAID OF YOUR BODY
WHEN YOUR BODY

My body is afraid of your body when your body
moves to move away. My body is a theme party
that's found a deeper way to care about its guests
and when they leave. It's me and not my body
that gets the words of the song wrong, *My body lies*
over the ocean, though it's my body that gets up now
to turn off the television. On it, two bodies who aren't
your body read news that pertains to other bodies
and are proper inside their clothing. I or is it my body
knows when it's time to make a room go dark, the trick
is sending the sound away. Sometimes when I'm trying
to fall asleep I picture large quantities of mercury.
It feels good to picture this, it all slows down.
Sometimes when things feel good, everything speeds up,
like when a body responds to the music at theme parties.
I wonder if you're having the same thought as I
am having now, that it's too quiet to be the world.

FIRST THINGS

First things turn me into
        something of a plow
every happening

loosened and chewed
        churned over
I root around

for a place to put
        between us
a thing about weather

it's hard on the ground
        tricked plants
unclench then stiffen

on a day like today
        with weather
I have you-thoughts

and to say they're *pushing*
        up out of the earth
like some crocus—who was it

who said in the move
        from deep nothing-
sleep into a sleep

with dreams the mind's
       like a well-fed seed
there are things

I sometimes remember
       there are things
I sometimes

remember as nonsense like
       the part where I'm a plow
or you are

in the morning
       even the morning
gets the season all wrong

until the sun comes out
       and kicks it
into rightness

IF I WERE TO RISE UP ALL COLORLESS,

I could gather up old thoughts the way
a mind distant in love brings about a gathering
of stars. I don't want people thinking

I don't care about the future. Plenty of people
are wrong about how I feel. For instance,
I bought a bar of soap to remind me

of a clean time coming, the smell of it.
Even I wasn't right about how I was feeling then.
Embattled by a sense of honor,

I plotted to bring the smell of Lysol
like metal on teeth straight into the future.
Some thoughts, being in them feels

like a battle to let a rare look inform me
of how delicate and uncrackable I am.
How like an egg I can just roll myself

under the heart in the exact right way,
let it exert its pressure on my poles
and never crush me. The stars,

a gathering of paper under which
we may be crushed. I was about to be proud.
I felt a late wish of pride unfurling.

When we arrive from distant cities cracked
with love I don't know if I'll want my new hands
to work any differently than the hands

I stashed in the drawer.
And yet by the smell of the gathering sky
I am arranged and disrupted!

»

*The Sages taught [...] a list of places where one is required to recite
a blessing due to miracles that were performed there: One who
sees the crossings of the Red Sea, where Israel crossed; and the
crossings of the Jordan; [...] and Lot's wife.*

*On all of these miracles one must give thanks and offer praise
before God.*

The Talmud, Berakhot 54a

»

LOT'S WIFE SPEAKS

*

Before turning
to look at what
you're not
supposed to see

there's a moment
when you realize
that you can

you have a neck
two eyes lithe
torso the body
a working case
in this case lifted
by another

on a little trip

just up over
these dunes

some future will
accommodate
your looking

now's an injunction
to follow

all you have to do
is allow yourself
by sight

to be lifted
sink
into the utility

of your shape

a body made
to be carried
off opened

*

To what degree
do I have to move
to be able to see

the flames

which portion
of this punishment
is the punishment

the loss of my own
moving limbs or feeling
stretched into looking

in the red smoke
I couldn't blink
but looked back

now I see endlessly

a child caught smoking
forced to smoke
until she's sick

is this an indulgence
so much looking

will I learn a lesson
as the city smolders

to block the sun
moon and sun again

I tire and I am
perpetually tired

what will grow up
around me will certainly
die or else learn
to live by my salt

learn to curl around
my salt ankles

to undo me will take
a punishment so severe
this time it will

by flood or by earthquake

against all covenant
undo the earth

*

Maybe the solution
to cleanse by fire
always required a witness

to prevent it from ever being
a solution

I was too late

to draw out a flush
on the face of a great god
ashamed of his own arrogance

that this could be the end of suffering
that this could possibly be the end of all suffering

that I alone in my late turning
am suddenly responsible

this yellowing ground
so much a part of me
I cannot flee from it

when the sea sits out long enough
in the sun

I am what's left

a mother without her children
has no one to be embarrassed for
but god

when the men came
I would not give up my daughters
now I'll never see them age

this new order of events
that I'll live to outlive
even the meaning of

*

At what was I meant to look
and never stop looking

compared to what
is this situation
pain

I'll never know death
though I see it coming
from across the plain

it rolls in like a storm
without a season

I am a storm
without a season

I never arrive
or depart

just hang here understanding nothing
but that I'll never leave the desert

or take anything ever again
in these hands

once I had a name

I was stilled before I could loosen it
the arrow from my mouth

*

Struck dumb in the desert
I imagine
in the future

there's no one left
to watch the wick of the sinner
burn long in its pit

where speech turns
to fire in the hole
silence is sacred

until upon this land
words from all over gather

like a story
or a way to tell it

mine is an eternity to consider

what occurs in front of me
where I can't move

is the present moment

men and their daughters
blown back into the walls

into the land I once felt
like a blessing
against my back

*

My questions are made like me
of salt and a lack of motion

Do we do any of our seeing for others

stillness which so many are seeking
I have at the very core of me

Do we ever do any of our actual seeing for others

a sudden arrangement of particulars
enters me

and I am urged

into a solid
looking column

*

Is my modern predicament
a desk
I never get up from

a news story I am compelled
to see repeating

like a body heating under the sun
at the outskirts of a violent village

I'm a warning

the future is coming
and we're all in it

dissolved until there is nothing
to watch us
but salt

when we're no longer seen
what do we become

or am I meant to prevent
future evil happenings
by bearing witness

in which case why is it not
those with evil in their hearts
that do the bearing

what is sitting too long at a desk
in the world without moving
what is a burden

to move and keep moving

to be taken
by the blast
by a stillness

by our looking

is it a burden, god

how
we may become changed

»

"She's got everything she needs, she's an artist, she don't look back."

Bob Dylan

»

THE FIELD YOU WEREN'T

I don't make many trips to the field anymore
don't pluck my words out from behind the ears
of white mushrooms and bring them to my mouth
just think of the field every now and then
as a place I used to find richly colored fruits
that fell to the ground that I could pretend
to pull out from behind your big ears
I don't know how big your ears are anymore
and I'll write this quickly to keep from remembering
I don't even run into that field now
for a quick glimpse though the thought sits
like a magnet sits nearby another magnet trembling
I read the ancient secret to controlling oneself
is never losing control of oneself
to begin not doing by never starting
you are never a field I walked into
now I return to the field you weren't
to remind myself of what never was like
before that brief beautiful break from it
before the never again again I found a prayer
in the field : let me be a lawnmower
or a door that's never heard of a field
that opens on a shed full of lawnmowers
and gravel in bags and serious-faced men
with contracts primed to pave

I AM SMALL

And still unclear
            is the quality
of my lostness
            to the visible stars
more visible
            in the desert
great literature
                love
places we wander
            concealing a slow tongue
where fear grows
              plantwild
the dark makes forms
            unknowable
I give thanks for not
                in this dry moment
having to answer for myself
            or forage for wheat
beneath the sky's great bravery
                  I must be a nettle
or else a tiny trophy bound
            by sand these feet
from time to time displaced
                gathered up
where I was found traversing
            in my actual steps
the length of my own
            brief name

SPECTATOR

Muath Safi Yousef al-Kasasbeh, 1988-2015

If what I see changes
me then I am changed
constantly I am a fire
in the cage I am the possibility
of seeing a fire in a cage
that creeps if fire creeps
towards the man in the video
who is preserved first as alive
and then as I can only imagine
an unimaginable shrieking
sound is preserved and shared
what is seeable is reaching out
what is reaching out I can see
at any moment I can choose this
burning distant execution
drawing near the clickable
the invasion of a man's
dying face in my home
I have nothing additional
to add to the world
my watching tonight
is permanent and will pass
under the moon gone
pale out of respect
for the way time takes us
with it despite our decisions
to see or not to see ourselves
inflicted on the viral wind
where our decisions drive

traffic headlong into future
versions of ourselves that rise
into the morning still
with living with

IT'S OKAY, CLARK KENT,
YOU'RE NOT FROM AROUND HERE

Anyway, it's better to hide in plain sight.
As in, I was born here with few abilities
but I can spend all my time learning to use them.
As in I am permitted by my position to leave
my exact position far behind and no one
will notice. My movements are small and make
tiny sparks. Now you've gone missing
like you're afraid we might decide to send you back.
Look, sometimes a super hero needs to lay low
on a beach somewhere. Sometimes a super hero
needs to say *I believe in how bad it all has to get*
before I am able to fix it. I believe in building places
where it's nearly impossible not to make something
good happen as long as there are a lot of us
present, for instance, a train before it starts
to move is a box of people thinking
about moving. Then it's a train pulling away.

IN A MUSEUM, I AM MOVED
TO CONTEMPLATE PACK ANIMALS

Lately I've been looking at things that hurt me.
Caring, as I do, not at all for art.

When a frame hangs its weight on a wall
I feel mostly for the wall.

Before carving, the sculptor remarks
the shape of his art inside the rock,
being that the rock is built by Time
and the Earth to carry the smooth musculature
of the beautiful thing I see in it, he says.

Some burdens are unfair.

It's the Saturday before Easter,
and the beginnings of something are percolating
somewhere in a cave, waiting for a rock
to roll away. That rock, likely, just a rock.

When you fall to your knees to tug your shoe up
over your heel your stacked bones groan
like a camel. Sad pack animal—no.

The camel's purpose is not to stir
the strange goings-out of the heart we call
empathy but to bear weight and even
to like it, probably, its whole body
down to its hard knee-joints tells me this.
No matter. I'll feel what I feel.

PLEASE
PLEASE ME

What am I getting at? Away?
I am the same pair of legs
as yesterday. When the sun sinks
they collapse against each other
like two spoons in a drawer. I don't
trust a single thing I can think of
as another thing. That determination
in the mind, where a word bank
supplants all that is knowable
with horses on the horizon,
steel girders, a scooter.
How are we supposed to know
what will happen without knowing
what will happen? Or maybe
I can see the future for real.
Once I said *you are the sand*
at my side before the sand,
the side. Or maybe we always
come true for one another.
The mind, digging in its shell.
How will I describe a metal color
all by myself? I'm asking.
I'm at the right spot to pause
for a question I know the
right answer to like I am
going to die? I can't look at
people in the eye unless
they love me and then I can't
look them in the eye.

WHITE SANDS

*

If in pieces we are accurate   is the initial question of composition
the we in question is made   of a transparent constituency
its parts cry out to be parts   together as parts
a vision of departing matters   when the parts take it up together
shifting over the tan plane   colors in a wide array
beyond the bank   white dunes tan dunes eggshell wedding dress
frosted in the light   sun up or down
the shifting marked in slowness   or too speedy to be looked directly at
if I were to follow the sun directly   if I were to whirl like what's left behind
in the water bucket   but I'm not alone here
knee deep in a soft evidence   of the particular
totality is   a triumph of the eye
the power I have   is a power to be overcome by vastness

*

The charge to always be ascending   even as you hold the landscape in place

is a purpose from which you might be freed   trees

the desert descends chromatic   into a predictable swirl

held up by the wind   the desert speaks of itself

in the third person   where it is possible to love

without water   water helps

am I best when buried   up to my ankles in something

in pieces   will I retain

my features   when setting up camp against the white sky

I could shuffle off into a bronze   just deep enough to be tragic

a melted color   on the edge of technology

a shift in the borders of a name   to include more parts

the way a dune is its only reasonable form   each time it takes shape

my morning features emerge   from the morning off-balance

and precarious   a dune blown back

*

When weather surrounds the basin between the dunes   singular
a storm field you can sit down in   with whatever bucket
a lightning rod passes   for memory
time and the body making its way   by the markers
the sand and the sky are double agents   have passports to blue
and to an unknown   transient clearness
their color describing the color   of what's around
stories don't compel me   their countless other people
dug up and transported to a site   of a whiter better beach
damaged by the digging up   telling is gradual
and impossible   like asking for forgiveness
in the middle of the act   betrayal has a solitary shape
in the mouth   behaving like a bucket
the land carved by ice and time   leaves nothing out
rotten with geometry   even the sand and sky
flatten their colors   against each other eager
to belong to more than one horizon   one of the great surprises of a life
is that you see   a great many things
before you die   it doesn't matter who you are

*

How long can a person in the sand   get away without learning

lamps are a challenge   in wind

just to live on top of the earth   until you blow away

seems simple enough   and brave

a small desert town the wind blows through   is like a small wind

like a streaker   swift and continuing

all the way to the center of town   the city shudders my element

out of itself   shrugs it off like a robe

before stepping into the bath   I am the opposite of rising

being in the car is a method   moving towards nighttime

where I can love almost   by accident

without anybody else seeing   to find the movement

of my own thoughts in the dark   first I must make it a home

dig my way through   to depiction

if depiction is to drive   headlong into what I'm seeing

we can only be described using words   we've used before

unless we invent new words   that's where a name comes in

a made-up word   for nothing's ever happened

quite like this   when it has

*

Beetles like tiny armored vehicles   define the sand

its defenses   the walk to camp

time's ribbon rolling out ahead of me   where I won't know

what kind of thing I am   about to be doing

there's no such thing as about to be   unfaithful

outside the bucket or in it   with two hands

the city is far away   the movement I am harboring

inside my body is typical   for a tree in the desert

typical the stars in their vividness   apart from the clouds

there's never a right way to drift   as when driving past the prison

I think *criminals*   doesn't consider circumstance

as granular   another city on a long stretch of empty road

appearing   as an oasis built by deprivation

technology makes   a present connection possible

though I've left love I am still   in my right mind

action and inaction   both a making up

of the mind   I make my bed like I make my behaviors

leaving others out of them   I lied

when I thought I brought the city with me   isn't that a kind of love

*

I'm still moving forward   when I exit the vehicle

road blind   considering what's ahead

it's not a bad place to be   out of my own hands

in the dry season   or a love that knows no next move

beyond repeating dunes sections   break apart

the horizon steady   by all rights

night drags its compass   by day

this feeling of not having made   my life what it is

even in its fullness of missing   conceals my every move

from me   I clear the debris

sand from the morning   and enter today's version

with more right than I know   what to do with

I am only ever myself   and that object

I sometimes speak from   the heart

I sometimes make   believe I am without

*

My possession of details is rudimentary   like a flower's

knowledge   the glass between myself and suffering

without me you wither   without knowing more about me you wither

more slowly   the dunes pasted to the horizon

this portion of land concealing   a made thing

like a kite hooking a cloud   with its reddest corner

love after a fashion   particular

stays buried   how catchy a hand in a sleeve

the string around the wrist   tugs of course

landscape enters   where love left the window loose

the song enters   I like it before I know what it is

I need what I don't know   to love

leaving out   I love

what I'm hearing as I'm driving   it's the only practice I have

the radio   green feelings

everything that can be killed is delicate   and is going to die

lace on a windshield   drives a fire in the ear

a change that's going to come   who among these seeing sounds

collides and can remain grateful   morning is a string

of unarticulated warm   cold wet dry feelings

when even the flowers   shake their heads

a fly reassuring on my arm   bruises the air

the sunrise never needs to try   to describe me

INNER RESOURCES

It feels good to love our country.
We must not say so. I'm divided by a love
of our millions of brilliant inventions
and how I'll dumbly sniff and rub each one
until I've figured out how I can use it for that
other thing. Just like a brilliant inventor I too
have a body so I know everything's invented
to pleasure a body. I was born to this country
and all of it was entranced by my tiny fingers
and then I learned where I could put them.
Before I was born there was sniffing and rubbing
and it formed a tiny unity. Already it was getting
too big to call by one name. It was becoming
a collection of purposes. Which is like calling the sky
a collection of purposes because stars exist.
This is why I write little notes to myself
reminding myself to take all the notes out
of my pockets before sleep. One note says look
at the sky and when I remember to do it I feel
very American. I feel American when I want
to be able to rub up against what I'm pretty sure
is that planet. Planets exist. They hold the names
we gave them inside them like a breath. I need
to remember to look up the names of the planets
I'm seeing. I'm fairly certain of what I'm seeing.
It's too bright to be anything else.

NOTES

I could not have written these poems without the thinking and
language present in books too numerous to mention, but I'm grateful
in particular for *Forgetting Lot's Wife* by Martin Harries, along with two
collections of essays edited by Tony Hillerman: *The Spell of New Mexico*
and *New Mexico, Rio Grande and Other Essays*.

The Biblical quotation is taken from *The Holy Scriptures According
to the Masoretic Text*, published by the Jewish Publication Society
of America; the Edmund Jabés quotation from *The Book of Questions*,
translated by Rosemarie Waldrop; and the Talmudic quotation from
the William Davidson Talmud.

"The Lightning Field" engages with a land art work of the same name
by Walter de María in Catron County, New Mexico.

"Industrial Cottage" takes after a painting of the same name by James
Rosenquist.

"If I Were to Rise Up All Colorless," borrows its title from Dante's *La
Vita Nuova*.

"My New Grief" and "A Problem with the Moon in It Is the Sky" are
for Eli Daniel Nemetz Todd.

"White Sands" begins with a phrase from a poem in Cole Swensen's
remarkable collection *Goest*: "if in pieces we are accurate".

"Inner Resources" owes a debt to John Berryman's "Dream Song 14."

THANK YOU

To the editors of the following publications, in which earlier versions of these poems first appeared: *Ampersand Review, The Awl, Barn Owl Review, Black Warrior Review, BOMB Magazine, Boston Review, Cincinnati Review, Colorado Review, Copper Nickel, Crazyhorse, Fanzine, Indiana Review, LIT, PEN America, Salt Hill, Sonora Review, Spark & Echo Arts, Timber, Tin House, Versal* and *Zone 3.*

To my teachers, too numerous to name. To Lisa Russ Spaar, for starting it. To Rita Dove, Charles Wright, Mark Doty, Nick Flynn, Tony Hoagland. To the writing and human communities at the University of Virginia and the University of Houston, where I first learned and relearned how to work. To the artists and makers and administrators at the Provincetown Fine Arts Work Center, the Wisconsin Institute for Creative Writing, the Helene Wurlitzer Foundation and Tent: Encounters with Jewish Culture for believing in these poems, and for providing much of the time and space and support it took to write them.

To the radical humans at Octopus Books for giving these words a home in the world. To Erik Carter and Desmond Wong and Christina Janus for turning a wish into a beautiful physical object.

To those people whose approaches to art-making and friendship have shaped my writing and my life, and kept me laughing through both. To Eric Kocher, Joe Chapman, Charlotte Hornsby, Julia Cohen, Molly Seltzer, Sara Yenke, David Moltz, Allison Cekala, Jack McGavick, Dane Wisher, Adam Peterson, Kent Shaw, Lisa Fay Coutley, Janine Joseph, Ed Porter, Ryler Dustin, Sean Bishop, Liz Countryman, Sam Amadon, Zac Fulton, Chloe Honum, sam sax, Sophia Starmack,

Cecily Scutt, April Freely, Rebecca Gayle Howell, Stephanie Soileau, Rachel Gelenius, Bridget Mullen, Alexandria Smith. To my vast and beautiful Young Writers Workshop family. To Margo Figgins for dreaming into being much of what has become my life. To Jenny Johnson for showing me a way. To Molly McCully Brown for our lifelong conversation. To Paul Erik Lipp for the Roadhouse. To Greg Brown for traveling with me. To my brother Jeff Martin for the night sky. To my brother Seth Engel for being my first best friend.

To Jonathan Ade, for a lifetime of friendship and support and laughter. You shape stories with your whole intelligent heart. Without you, this book wouldn't be.

To my family. To Mamma-Wendy Saz and John Dean for believing in this, and in me.

And to Mike Devine, my one house, my home. Thank you for everything, most of all.